Coasts

Melanie Waldron

www.heinemann.co.uk/library

Visit our website to find out more information about Heinemann Library books.

To order:
- ☎ Phone 44 (0)1865 888066
- 🖹 Send a fax to 44 (0)1865 314091
- 🖥 Visit the Heinemann Library Bookshop at www.heinemann.co.uk/library to browse our catalogue and order online.

First published in Great Britain by Heinemann Library, Halley Court, Jordan Hill, Oxford OX2 8EJ, part of Harcourt Education. Heinemann Library is a registered trademark of Harcourt Education Ltd.

Editorial: Joanna Talbot
Design: Richard Parker and Q2A Solutions
Illustrations: Jeff Edwards
Picture Research: Hannah Taylor
Production: Duncan Gilbert

Originated by Chroma Graphics (Overseas) Pte. Ltd
Printed and bound in China by Leo Paper Group

ISBN 978 0 431 10992 3
11 10 09 08 07
10 9 8 7 6 5 4 3 2 1

British Library Cataloguing in Publication Data
Waldron, Melanie
Coasts. – (Mapping Earthforms)
551.4'57

A full catalogue record for this book is available from the British Library.

Acknowledgements

The publishers would like to thank the following for permission to reproduce photographs: Alamy Images/David Wall p. **11**; Corbis pp. **15** (Bill Ross), **10** (Steve Terrill), **5** (Torleif Svensson), **23** (Yann Arthus-Bertrand), **7** (zefa/Theo Allofs); FLPA/D P Wilson p. **8**; Getty Images/Stone p. **27**; naturepl.com pp. **19** (Ben Osborne), **18** (Christophe Courteau); NHPA pp. **16** (Alberto Nardi), **17** (Jim Bain); Photolibrary pp. **4** (Pacific Stock), **26** (Photononstop); Science Photo Library pp. **20** (Peter Bowater), **9** (William Ervin); Skyscan/J Farmarp p. **13**; Still Pictures pp. **12** (Jeff Greenburg), **24** (Pierre Zeni).

Cover photograph reproduced with permission of Lonely Planet/ Richard I'Anson

Every effort has been made to contact copyright holders of any material reproduced in this book. Any omissions will be rectified in subsequent printings if notice is given to the publishers.

Contents

Any words appearing in the text in bold, **like this**, are explained in the Glossary. You can find the answers to Map Active questions on page 29.

What is a coast?

Think of a place where the land meets the sea. You might think of a sunny, sandy beach where the waves gently wash on to the shore. You might think of a steep, rocky cliff with huge, white waves crashing against black rocks. Both of these places are coasts. Coasts are everywhere that the land and sea meet.

There are many different types of coasts all over the world. But they all have one thing in common – the sea. All coasts are affected by waves and **tides**, and all coasts change because of the sea. This might be every day, as the tides come in or go out. It could be over hundreds of years, as the sea **erodes** the land. The powerful action of the sea means that coasts are the world's most rapidly changing landforms.

▼ The sea can be very powerful and can attack the coastline. Hard rock can resist this attack, but softer rock will soon give way.

▲ Coasts can be very busy places! Most people love to spend time by the sea. However, this means that coasts can sometimes be badly affected by human activity.

How have coasts formed?

For the last 6,000 years, sea levels across the world have been stable. Coastlines have been developing and changing around the edges of all the great **continents** of the world. The coastlines we see today have formed during this time. They are a result of the **interaction** between the land and the sea. In some places the sea washes the land away, and in others it builds up the land.

Life at the coast

There are many different types of plants and animals living at the coast. Many of these have **adapted** to living in the narrow strip of land where it meets the sea. Plants and animals have done this in order to survive in this changing environment. Humans also live and work at the coast, and we are affecting coastlines all around the world.

Coasts of the world

Coasts are found all over the world, wherever a land mass meets the sea. Most countries in the world have a bit of coastline, but some do not. There are 43 countries that are **landlocked**, such as Paraguay in South America. This means that they do not have any land that borders the sea. All other countries have at least part of their borders meeting the sea. Some countries, such as Iceland, are completely surrounded by the sea. The whole border is made up of coastline.

In some countries, the coastline can change quickly over a short distance. In the United Kingdom, for example, some parts of the south coast change from rocky cliffs to flat bays, concrete sea defences, and shingle beaches in less than 50 kilometres (31 miles). In other parts of the world, however, the same type of coast can stretch for long distances. The Skeleton Coast in Namibia, for example, is a huge area of sand and sea that stretches for more than 500 kilometres (310 miles) up the west African coast.

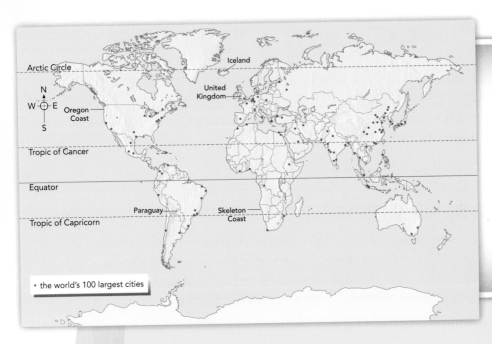

Arctic Circle
Iceland
N
W ⊕ E
S
United Kingdom
Oregon Coast
Tropic of Cancer
Equator
Paraguay
Skeleton Coast
Tropic of Capricorn

• the world's 100 largest cities

◀ Most of the world's largest cities are found very close to the coast. One reason is because access to the sea can increase the sea trade in and out.

MAP ACTIVE

Can you identify any areas in the world where there are no large cities near the coast? Think of some reasons for this.

The most important factors in shaping the coastline are the rock that the land is made of, and the direction and power of the waves. Very hard rocks, such as granite, will be able to resist attack from powerful waves, although over time they will eventually **erode**. When hard rocks erode they can leave behind some amazing landforms. Soft rock, such as clay, will be easily eroded by waves. The coastline can quickly move inwards as the land erodes. The material that has been eroded can be moved along the coast and change the coastline there.

In very cold areas of the world such as northern Russia, where the land and sea are covered with ice, it is quite difficult to tell where the coastline actually is. Only in summer, when some of the ice has melted, are parts of the coastline revealed.

▲ The Skeleton Coast in Namibia is so called because of the dangerous rocks and powerful waves that lie off the shore. Many ships have been wrecked along this coast.

Tides and waves

Tides

Every coastline around the world is affected by the changing **tide**. The tide is the rise and fall in the surface of the sea. Twice every day, the sea level is high and the sea washes higher up the land. This is called **high tide**. As soon as it reaches high tide, the sea starts to drop down again until it reaches its lowest level. This is called **low tide**, and the sea does not wash far up the land. Low tides also occur twice every day.

high tide

low tide

▲ Plants and animals living in the area between high tide and low tide are specially **adapted**. They need to cope with being under the sea for half their lives.

The tides are created by the pull of the Moon's **gravity** on the sea. As the Moon orbits Earth it pulls a bulge of water with it, and this creates the tides. The difference in height between high tide and low tide can be large, depending on the position of the Moon and the shape of the coastline. In some places the difference can be more than 10 metres (33 feet).

▲ As waves head towards the coast, the bottom of the wave begins to drag on the ground below the sea. This makes the top of the wave "topple over" (break).

Waves

The surface of the sea is rarely smooth and still. This is because of waves. Waves are created by winds blowing over the sea's surface. Stronger winds create higher, more powerful waves with lots of energy. The waves can build up in height and energy if the wind blows in the same direction over a large distance. We call this distance the **fetch**. The longer the fetch is, the larger the wave.

Waves can have a huge effect on the coast. Small waves with little energy wash gently up the land. These waves do not create much **erosion**. However, large waves with lots of energy can crash on to the land, breaking up bits of rock and moving them around. The wind, and the size and power of the waves, can change a coast from a calm and peaceful place to a wild and dangerous one.

Erosion at the coast

Waves and erosion

Where waves break on the coast, they can cause **erosion** of rock. The amount of erosion depends on the height and strength of the waves, and also on the type of rock.

There are different types of erosion:
- **Abrasion**. Waves can contain particles of sand and **shingle**. When the waves hit the rock, the particles can wear the rock away.
- **Wave pounding**. When strong, high waves slam against the rock, the energy of the wave produces a shock wave through the rock. This can cause it to weaken and eventually break up.
- **Hydraulic pressure**. Little holes and cracks on the surface of rocks have air inside them. This air can become **compressed** when the waves hit the rocks. The trapped air can cause the cracks to get bigger, and this breaks up the rock.
- **Corrosion**. Some types of rock, such as limestone, dissolve in salty seawater. Over time the rock gets worn further and further back.

Landforms caused by erosion

Erosion at the coast can create some spectacular landforms. **Headlands** and **bays** are created when the rock type changes from hard to soft along the coast. Headlands are sections of hard rock, such as granite, that stick out into the sea. Bays in between the headlands are areas of soft rock and clay that have been more easily **eroded**.

▶ The sea has eroded the rock near Crook Point in Oregon to leave behind these amazing formations.

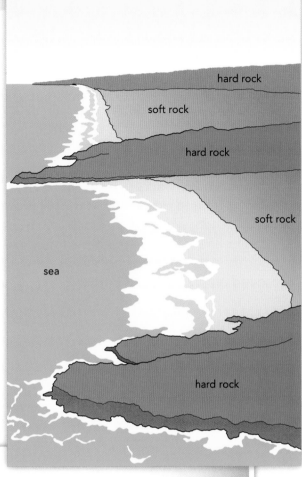

▲ At Noosa Head in Queensland, Australia, the sea has eroded the soft rock to form bays. The harder rock has resisted erosion to form headlands. This clearly shows that the rock type has a great effect on the shape of the coast.

Wave-cut platforms are found at the bottom of coastal cliffs. They are created when the waves erode the bottom of the cliff, and the cliff above eventually collapses. Over time the cliff is pushed further and further back, leaving a flat platform of rock that is exposed at low tide.

The most amazing coastal landforms include caves, **arches**, and **stacks**. All of these are created over long periods of time as waves gradually erode more and more material. Caves can be worn through to the other side, leaving an archway. If the rock at the top of the archway collapses, this leaves a stack standing on its own in the sea.

Deposition at the coast

Longshore drift

When rocks are **eroded**, the small particles that break off can be carried in the waves. Over time, these particles get worn and rounded to form sand or **shingle**. This can be picked up by waves and moved along the coast.

Longshore drift occurs when waves hit the coast at an angle, instead of straight up and down. Any material picked up by the waves is moved up the beach. Then, when it runs back down the beach, the sea always runs in a straight line rather than at an angle. This means that material is not moved back to its original position. Over time this causes lots of material to be moved along the beach.

▼ Longshore drift can build up material in some places, but in other places material is constantly being removed. On some beaches, **beach replenishment** can help to reduce the effects of this.

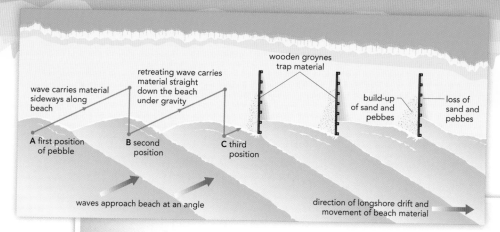

wave carries material sideways along beach

retreating wave carries material straight down the beach under gravity

wooden groynes trap material

build-up of sand and pebbes

loss of sand and pebbes

A first position of pebble

B second position

C third position

waves approach beach at an angle

direction of longshore drift and movement of beach material

▲ Longshore drift moves material along a beach until a barrier stops the material, or until the coast changes shape and the waves no longer approach at an angle.

Landforms of deposition

When particles of sand and shingle are dropped by waves, we call this **deposition**. This happens when waves reach more sheltered areas of coast, where they lose their energy and can no longer carry the material. Deposition can create some beautiful landforms.

Spits are long, narrow stretches of sand and shingle. They are joined to the coastal land at one end. They are created when beach material is moved along the coast until it reaches areas where the coast changes shape and the wave energy drops. A spit that reaches another section of coastal land is called a **bar**.

A **tombolo** is a stretch of sand and shingle that joins an offshore island to the mainland. It is created when the waves break against the sea side of the island, then curve around the island. As the waves curve around they lose their energy, and the material is dropped where the waves have the lowest energy.

Barrier islands are made of deposited sand and shingle. They form long stretches of islands running alongside the coastline. Often **salt marshes** build up behind these islands. Salt marshes are areas of deposited mud, **silt**, and sand that have been built up high enough to allow specially **adapted** plants to grow.

▶ Dawlish Warren in Devon, UK, is a spit which has been built up over hundreds of years. The sea is constantly moving material along the coast.

The Oregon Coast

The state of Oregon lies on the western side of the United States. The coastline of Oregon stretches for 476 kilometres (296 miles) along the Pacific Ocean. There are some sandy beaches along the coast, but it is most famous for its rocky cliffs and shores. Lighthouses are placed all along the coast to warn ships about these rocks.

Erosion has played a large part in shaping the Oregon coast. There are rocky **headlands**, sea **stacks**, **arches**, and caves. In the central part there are large **sand dunes**, formed by the wind blowing sand into huge mounds.

Coastal wildlife

There are many different **species** of plants and animals living along the Oregon Coast. Sea lions, seals, whales, and porpoises make their homes in the coastal waters. Seabirds such as the tufted puffin and the western gull feed on the rich variety of small sea life. The **tide pools** contain a whole range of animals from sea urchins to crabs. Plant life includes the coastal strawberry (a type of rose) and the beach daisy.

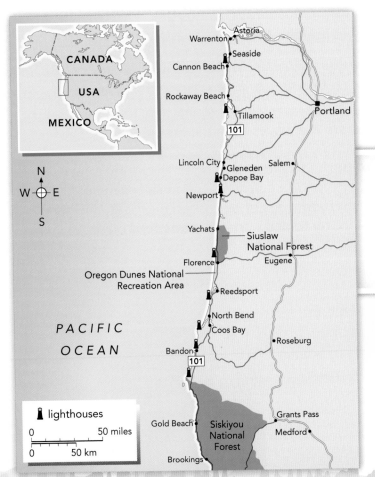

◀ The Oregon Coast is lined with both protected areas and towns.

▲ Cannon Beach on the Oregon Coast is a fine example of the rocky natural beauty of the area.

People of the Oregon Coast

More than 10,000 years ago, Native Americans settled along the coast. They fished the seas using wooden canoes, and hunted the land near by. After Europeans began visiting and trading in the 1700s, the first permanent town, Astoria, was built in the early 1800s. Soon settlements were being built all along the coast, as people took advantage of the good farming land, the rich timber forests, and the growing salmon-fishing industry.

Today tourism is a very important industry on the Oregon Coast. Tourists come to see the spectacular natural rock formations along the coast, to laze on sandy beaches, and to visit old fishing villages and bigger resorts. More energetic activities are also on offer – including surfing, boating, scuba-diving, fishing, cycling, and hiking. However, there is a downside to the popularity of the area. There is only one major road, Highway 101, that runs the length of the coastline, and traffic jams are very common. In fact, the area has been named as having the worst tourist traffic in the United States.

Coastal plants

All plants growing at the coast have to cope with some fairly harsh conditions. Plants that grow where seawater sometimes covers the land must be able to grow in salty water. On many coasts there are strong winds, and these winds can pick up salty spray from the sea that is then blown on to plant leaves. Plants have **adapted** to living and growing in these environments.

▲ Coastal vegetation has adapted to deal with changing tides, salty air and water, and strong winds.

Halophytes

In coastal areas where **silt** is deposited, for example where a river meets the sea, plants can grow on the **mudflats** that form. These areas of mud are located in what is known as the **intertidal zone** (the land that is exposed at **low tide**, but covered by the sea at **high tide**). Plants that grow here are called **halophytes**. Halophytes can survive in salty conditions that would kill other plants. Halophytes include saltbush and cordgrass.

▲ Halophytes such as this Marsh Samphire have adapted to living in very salty conditions. Marsh Samphire can be eaten. It is washed carefully and then boiled in water for around ten minutes.

Halophytes can control the balance of salt in their tissues in two main ways. Some plants are called excluders, and they have special **cells** inside them that can collect the salt and "sweat" it through the plant's leaves. Other plants are called includers. These plants store large quantities of water inside their cells so that the impact of the salt is reduced.

Sand dune vegetation

Most **sand dunes** have vegetation growing on them. This helps to hold the dunes together. Dunes that build high enough can provide shelter for vegetation behind them. A very common sand dune plant is marram grass. Marram grass can cope very well with strong coastal winds. It grows quite low to the surface and its leaves can fold to reduce their surface area. It also has very long roots to reach supplies of water deep under the sand dunes.

Coastal animals

Many different kinds of animals make their homes along coastlines. Although the animals have to cope with salty water, crashing waves, and high winds, the coast provides rich food and a variety of different **habitats**.

In the **intertidal zone**, animals have **adapted** in many ways. They have adapted to:

- Moisture levels: Sometimes the sea covers the land, at other times it is exposed to the air. Animals must cope with both wet and dry conditions. Animals such as crabs can breathe under the water using **gills**. As long as these gills are kept moist when the crab is out of the water, they can take oxygen from the air and keep the crab alive.
- Moving water: When the tide comes in, powerful waves can crash on to the shore and back again. Animals must be able to withstand this moving water. They do this by burrowing into the sand, like clams, or attaching themselves to rocks, like barnacles.
- Salt water: Some animals have special, thin layers of skin called membranes that can control the amount of salt that passes through into the animals' bodies.

▶ Once the tide has gone out you can see a huge variety of animals that make their homes along the coastline.

Seabirds

Some seabirds, such as the oystercatcher and the egret, are known as wading birds. They are called this because they wade out into the intertidal zone and search for worms and molluscs buried in the sand and mud. Other birds live perched on rocky cliffs high above the sea. Here they build nests and raise their young on fish caught in the sea. Gannets have developed an amazing diving technique. They rise into the air and then plunge into the water, catching fish near the surface.

Mammals at the coast

Many different **mammals** live at the coast. Most of them, such as otters, seals, and walruses, spend large parts of their lives in the sea. They come ashore to rest, sleep, give birth, and nurse their pups. Other mammals, such as rabbits and mice, live among the thick coastal vegetation. Rabbits prefer light, sandy coastlines where they can easily dig out burrows.

▲ These kittiwakes and guillemots bring up their young on tiny narrow ledges on the cliff face. They must nest close to the sea so that they can find enough fish to feed their chicks.

Living at the coast

Humans have settled in coastal areas for thousands of years. There have been huge benefits to living at the coast. The earliest settlements grew up because of the plentiful supply of fish and other seafood to be found at the coast and in the sea. Also, in some countries, such as Japan, the inland areas are mostly mountainous, so good flat land for settling on was found around the coast.

Later, when sea travel and trade became widespread, it made sense to settle by the coast because goods could be bought and sold here. To help this trade, shipbuilding industries and ports began to grow in coastal areas. This also increased the amount of coastal settlement. A large proportion of today's important cities are on the coast, and have grown from settlements that grew up hundreds of years ago.

Leisure time

Today, the coast is a major attraction for tourists and for local people who like to spend their leisure time there. Industries and companies have taken advantage of this. They have built hotels, apartments, shops, restaurants, and amusements. Many activity companies have set up at the coast, for example diving schools, windsurfer hire shops, marinas, and boat trip organisations.

▼ Shipping and fishing are still important industries for towns and cities across the world, such as in Hong Kong in China.

Case study – Mombasa

Mombasa is Kenya's largest coastal settlement and second largest city, after Nairobi. It sits in the southeast of Kenya on the Indian Ocean coast, and has a population of around 500,000 people.

The city grew as an important trade centre in the 1500s. At this time the Portuguese had a lot of control over the area, and they built some of Mombasa's famous sites, such as Fort Jesus. This fort was used as a trading site, as a prison, and to protect the Portuguese when conflicts with local people arose. After about 200 years the Portuguese control was taken over by Arab communities in the area. Slavery was the main trade out of Mombasa until the 1900s. Spices, cotton, and coffee were also traded.

Today, Mombasa is a major tourist destination. The beaches to the north and south of the city are beautiful and development has been limited to protect some of the natural coastal **habitats**.

▶ Mombasa city centre is located on an island on the Kenyan coast.

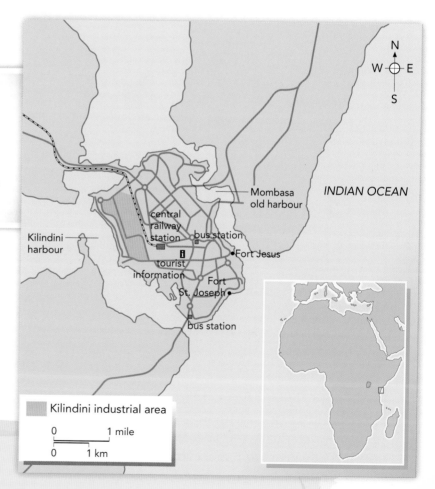

MAP ACTIVE

Why do you think the city grew on an island? What problems might this cause in modern times?

A way of life – Iceland

The country of Iceland lies in the northern part of the Atlantic Ocean, between Norway and Greenland. Because the island is very volcanic and mountainous, with large areas covered in glaciers, most of the population of around 300,000 people live around the coast. Iceland's capital city, Reykjavik, is on the southwest coast.

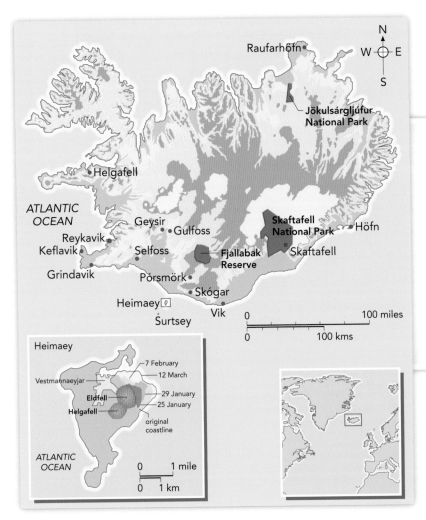

◄ Iceland and Heimaey, showing Heimaey's expanding coastline after the 1973 eruption. The grey areas are huge ice sheets and glaciers.

People from Norway first settled in Iceland about AD 870. In AD 930 they set up the world's first parliament, called the Althing. Fishing and farming were the main industries in the country's history, although at times food had to be imported because the harsh **climate** meant that producing food was very difficult. Today, fishing and fish processing are still the main industries and much of Iceland's international trade is based on its fish and fish products. Around 20 per cent of the population are employed in the fishing industry in some way.

The coastline of Iceland is **evolving**. Iceland sits on top of the Mid-Atlantic Ridge, a huge **faultline** on Earth's surface. This means that volcanic eruptions are frequent. On Heimaey, a small island to the south of the main island, a volcanic eruption in 1973 poured ash and lava over the surface of the island. It eventually ran out to the coast and built a new coastline when the lava cooled. Just a few years earlier, in 1963, an underwater volcano erupted and the lava built up to create a whole new island, called Surtsey.

Today, tourism is very important to Iceland. People come to visit the glaciers, the volcanoes, the hot springs, and the beautiful coasts all around. There are stunning **bays** and **fjords** along the coast, and in the south there are also sandy beaches. The total length of the coastline is almost 5,000 kilometres (3,000 miles).

▲ The inland area of Iceland is mountainous and very cold. Most human settlement and activity in Iceland takes place along the narrow, flat coast of the island.

Our changing coasts

Most of our coasts are changing all the time. The sea is an enormously powerful factor in shaping Earth, and coasts are continually being affected. Some dramatic changes are taking place where the sea is **eroding** the coast. These changes can be disastrous, such as when a huge section of sea cliff suddenly collapses after being weakened by **erosion**. This can have devastating results for people who have homes on cliff tops. For example, the Holderness coast on the eastern side of the United Kingdom is badly affected by erosion. The coast is estimated to be retreating by an average of about 2 metres (6 feet) per year. Many cliff-top buildings have fallen into the sea.

▶ Coastal erosion in Bonifacio, Corsica, has left these houses sitting precariously on top of a cliff. One day the cliff may collapse, taking the houses with it.